I do actually have some hobbies, but none worth talking about. Just little things that I dabble in.

In short, *Dragon Ball* is the only thing I can talk to people about.

—Toyotarou, 2020

Toyotarou

Toyotarou created the manga adaptation for the *Dragon Ball Z* anime's 2015 film, *Dragon Ball Z: Resurrection F*. He is also the author of the spin-off series *Dragon Ball Heroes: Victory Mission*, which debuted in *V-Jump* in Japan in November 2012.

Akira Toriyama

Renowned worldwide for his playful, innovative storytelling and humorous, distinctive art style, Akira Toriyama burst onto the manga scene in 1980 with the wildly popular *Dr. Slump*. His hit series *Dragon Ball* (published in the U.S. as *Dragon Ball* and *Dragon Ball Z*) ran from 1984 to 1995 in Shueisha's *Weekly Shonen Jump* magazine. He is also known for his design work on video games such as *Dragon Quest*, *Chrono Trigger*, *Tobal No. 1* and *Blue Dragon*. His recent manga works include *COWA!*, *Kajika*, *Sand Land*, *Neko Majin*, *Jaco the Galactic Patrolman* and a children's book, *Toccio the Angel*. He lives with his family in Japan.

DRAGON BALL SUPER 12

SHONEN JUMP Manga Edition

STORY BY **Akira Toriyama**
ART BY **Toyotarou**

TRANSLATION **Caleb Cook**
LETTERING **Brandon Bovia**
DESIGN **Joy Zhang**
EDITOR **Rae First**

DRAGON BALL SUPER © 2015 BY BIRD STUDIO, Toyotarou
All rights reserved. First published in Japan in 2015 by SHUEISHA Inc., Tokyo.
English translation rights arranged by SHUEISHA Inc.

The stories, characters and incidents mentioned
in this publication are entirely fictional.

Printed in Italy

Published by VIZ Media, LLC
P.O. Box 77010
San Francisco, CA 94107

10 9 8 7 6 5
First printing, March 2021
Fifth printing, February 2024

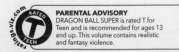

PARENTAL ADVISORY
DRAGON BALL SUPER is rated T for
Teen and is recommended for ages 13
and up. This volume contains realistic
and fantasy violence.

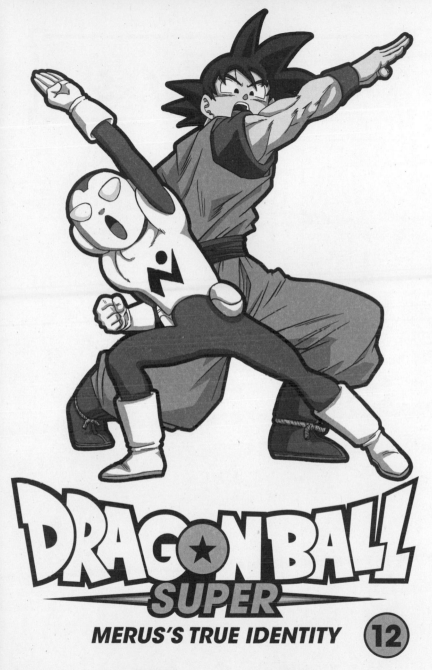

DRAGON BALL SUPER

SUPER

MERUS'S TRUE IDENTITY

12

STORY BY
Akira Toriyama

ART BY
Toyotarou

CAST OF
CHARACTERS

Guide Angel Whis

Piccolo

Kuririn

Son Goku

Vegeta

Pybara

Jaco

Bulma

Galactic Patrol
Agent: Irico

Esca

Moro

Escaped
Convict:
Pasta

Escaped
Convict:
Saganbo

Galactic Patrol Agent:
Merus

STORY THUS FAR

A long, long time ago, Son Goku left on a journey in search of the legendary Dragon Balls—a set of seven balls that, when gathered, would summon the dragon Shenlong to grant any wish. After a great adventure, he collects them all. Later, he becomes the apprentice of Kame-Sen'nin, fights a number of vicious enemies, defeats the great Majin Boo and restores peace on Earth. Some time passes, and then Lord Beerus, the God of Destruction, suddenly awakens and sets out in search of the Super Saiyan God. Goku, by becoming the Super Saiyan God, manages to stop Beerus from destroying the Earth and starts training under him with Vegeta. After some time, the ancient villain Moro escapes from the Galactic Prison and goes off to search for the Dragon Balls in new Namek, where Goku and the Galactic Patrol confront him. However, Moro's ability to absorb life energy is too much for them, and Moro manages to make his wishes. After retreating, Goku travels to a distant planet to train with Merus, while Vegeta goes to Yardrat to learn about spirit techniques that could defeat Moro. Meanwhile, Moro himself has freed a gang of convicts from the Galactic Prison and is commanding them to attack planets across the galaxy. Now, his evil may threaten Earth as well...

12 DRAGON BALL SUPER

TABLE OF CON-TENTS

DRAGON BALL SUPER

CHAPTER 53: SAGANBO'S GALACTIC BANDIT BRIGADE

THAT'S A LOT TO TAKE IN!!

HUUUH?

ON THAT NOTE, WHERE ARE GOHAN AND TENSHINHAN?

SO YOU SEE, THE GALACTIC PATROL NEEDS ALL THE FIGHTERS IT CAN GET.

GEEZ, WHO DOESN'T HAVE A PHONE IN THIS DAY AND AGE.

AND TENSHINHAN DOESN'T OWN A CELL PHONE, SO WE'VE GOT NO WAY TO REACH HIM.

GOHAN'S AT ONE OF HIS COLLEGE LECTURES, BUT HE'LL SWING BY AFTER THAT.

JACO'S HERE.

SHOOM

SHOULD WE CONTACT YAMCHA?

I TOLD YOU TO GATHER UP **ALL** THE TOUGHEST WARRIORS!

HEY, BULMA.

WHRRR

DENDE!!

I'M NOT **THAT** FREE...

KURIRIN WAS THE ONLY ONE WHO COULD COME. HE'S GOT ABSOLUTELY NOTHING ELSE GOING ON.

THE BRAT TAGGED ALONG WHEN I SAID I WAS HEADING FOR EARTH.

YES!

THANK GOODNESS YOU'RE SAFE!

IT'S REALLY YOU!

ESCA!

SO IF THERE'S ANY WAY I CAN HELP, PLEASE LET ME KNOW!

I'M READY TO FIGHT FOR PEACE IN THE GALAXY! AND TO RESTORE NAMEK!

...

WAS HE THE ONLY ONE WHO MADE IT?

YEP. YOU THREE ARE THE LAST SURVIVING NAMEKIANS.

HA HA HA... AS IF YOU LOSERS COULD EVER STAND UP TO MORO.

YOU THREE ARE THE LAST PEOPLE I EXPECTED TO RUN INTO HERE!!

LONG TIME NO SEE, PIP-SQUEAK.

IT'S OBEY OR BE KILLED-- NO THIRD OPTION, Y'HEAR?

PASTA!

...YOU'RE HEADED RIGHT BACK TO THE GALACTIC SLAMMER!

ONCE EVERY-THING'S HUNKY-DORY AGAIN...

MIGHTY KIND OF YOU TO SAY.

UGH, I'VE NEVER MET ANYONE WHO BELONGED IN A CAGE MORE THAN YOU.

YOU LET THEM CONTACT MORO?!

WHAT ?!

HA HA HA, YOU STILL DON'T GET IT--THE MAIN FORCE IS GONNA SWOOP DOWN TO RESCUE US ANY DAY NOW.

T-TRY LEADING WITH THAT NEXT TIME!

I'D BETTER ASK HQ TO CONFIRM WHO EXACTLY'S COMING OUR WAY!

NOD

NEVER HEARD OF IT... HOW 'BOUT YOU, YUNBA?

"EARTH"? HMM...

IT'S BEEN NOTHING BUT THESE STINKIN' BAR THINGS SINCE WE BUSTED OUTTA PRISON!

OF COURSE!

YOU'VE GOT FOOD ON THE BRAIN AND NOT MUCH ELSE, HUH?

BUT I SURE HOPE IT'S GOT YUMMY TREATS.

NOPE, SHIMO-REKKA.

THIRD PLANET FROM ITS STAR, IN THE OUTSKIRTS OF THE NORTHERN SECTOR OF SPACE.

PLANET 4032 GREEN-877.

12

DATA INDICATES THIS PLANET IS STILL IN THE DEVELOPMENTAL STAGE AND IS OF LITTLE VALUE.

SHOULDA KNOWN YOU'D HAVE THE INTEL, SEVEN-THREE.

HOWEVER, THIS DATA IS FROM BEFORE WE WERE ARRESTED BY THE GALACTIC PATROL. IT COULD BE OUT OF DATE.

PROLLY NOTHING YUMMY THEN...

LITTLE VALUE?

JUST A QUICK STOP!

FINE. WHATEVER.

SOUNDS LIKE A BORING ROCK.

BAH...

NO MORE WAITING!! FIND ANOTHER PLANET FOR A PIT STOP!

GAH! I'M SO HUNGRY!

TCH...

ALONG WITH OG73-1.

SCANS SUGGEST THAT SHIMOREKKA AND YUNBA ARE ON BOARD.

AGENT JACO! WE HAVE A READ ON THE SHIP CHARTING A COURSE FOR EARTH.

S-SEVEN-THREE IS WITH THEM?!

THEY RAMPAGED AROUND THE GALAXY BEFORE GREAT PAINS WERE TAKEN TO CATCH THEM.

THEY'RE MEMBERS OF AN INFAMOUS BRIGADE OF GALACTIC BANDITS.

ALL THREE ARE SAGAN-BO'S HENCHMEN.

IS THAT HIS NAME?

WHO THE HECK'S THAT?

...

NO. BY AGENT MERUS.

BY YOU, JACO?

14

IF YOU SURVIVE, I'LL BE BACK TO RECRUIT YOU LATER.

ON THAT NOTE, I'LL BE OFF.

VHRRR

W-WAIT A SECOND!

OH, SURE!

BUT THE EARTH'S GOT PICCOLO AND GOHAN... WE'LL BE FINE, RIGHT?

BUT TO BE HONEST? YEAH. EXACTLY.

YOU DON'T BEAT AROUND THE BUSH, HUH?

SO YOU'RE SAYING THEY'RE TOO STRONG FOR YOU TO BEAT.

YOU SHOULD STAY AND FIGHT TOO!

LEAVING SO SOON?!

AT LEAST TELL US THAT BEFORE YOU LEAVE.

WHAT DO WE NEED TO KNOW ABOUT THEM?

I ONLY CAME TO PICK UP THE NEW RECRUITS ANYWAY!

NAH! I'M OUTTA HERE!

YOU'RE THE ONLY ONE WHO KNOWS ANYTHING ABOUT THESE BADDIES! SO YOU'D BETTER HELP US!

BUT THEN I'M GONE.

SH-SHEESH, FINE.

...IS OG73-1 AND HIS NASTY SPECIAL MOVE.

THEY'RE ALL WICKED STRONG, BUT THE ONE TO WATCH OUT FOR...

GRAP

FWK FWK FWK

SHNK SHNK SHNK

SHP

FWAH

SKWEEZ

SO THIS ISN'T ABOUT HIJACKING BODIES OR BRAINWASHING?

A WHOLE HALF HOUR?

HE CAN STEAL OTHER PEOPLE'S POWERS BY GRABBING THEIR NECKS. THE STOLEN POWERS LAST FOR 30 MINUTES.

A **COPY ABILITY**?! WHAT DO YOU MEAN?

AN ARTIFICIAL ONE, COOKED UP BY A PLANET WITH ADVANCED TECH AND SCIENCE. SO HE'S GOT NOTHING RESEMBLING NORMAL EMOTIONS OR FEELINGS.

WHAT SORT OF BEING IS HE?

SEVEN-THREE'S ALREADY PLENTY STRONG, SO THE ABILITIES HE COPIES JUST GIVE HIM AN EXTRA BOOST.

NAH, NOT LIKE THAT.

HE'S JUST A KILLING MACHINE WHO OBEYS HIS ALLIES' ORDERS.

ZOOM ZOOM

HOW ABOUT YOU, PIC-COLO?

I NEVER STOP HONING MYSELF EVEN IN THE BEST OF TIMES.

ONLY TEN DAYS? I'D BETTER START TRAINING...

THEY'LL BE HERE IN ABOUT TEN DAYS.

WELL, HOW LONG DO WE HAVE?

20

S-SEV...

HUH?
WHO'RE
THEY?

THESE THREE ARE THE BANDITS?!

W-WHAT?!

SEVEN-THREE!!

LUCKY US-- THE PLANET WE STOPPED ON WAS HOME TO THESE CRITTERS WHO COULD CREATE WARP PORTALS.

WOULD'VE TAKEN DAYS TO GET HERE BY SPACESHIP.

H-H-HEY, STOP IN THE NAME OF THE LAW!

THE MACARENI GANG.

THERE.

DON'T TELL ME **YOU** WRANGLED THE MACARENI GANG?

IT'S JACO.

NOT A BAD DAY'S WORK!

RIGHT, RIGHT. WHY'RE YOU HERE, GUY?

OH? YOU'RE WITH THE GALACTIC PATROL, YEAH?

DRAWING A BLANK ON YOUR NAME THOUGH...

BE A PAL AND BUST US OUTTA HERE?

YOU SHOWED UP QUICK, SHIMO-REKKA!

AND IF YOU'RE HERE TO SAVE THEM, THINK AGAIN!!

D-DARN RIGHT I DID!!

...

?

I'VE GOT A MESSAGE FOR YOU FROM LORD MORO.

ALIVE AND WELL, HUH?

HEYA, PASTA!

HIS WORDS, NOT MINE.

SHOOM

TRAITORS WHO ACT ON THEIR OWN ARE DISPOSABLE.

GRP

24

GAH!!

PICCOLO!!

ACK!

FWAH

SKWEEZ

ZRRG

TCH!

....!

HEH HEH... YOU'VE GOT SOME SWEET MOVES UP YOUR SLEEVE, I GUESS.

YOU LET HIM COPY ALL YOUR ABILITIES !!

WHAT ?!

28

29

JACO !!

AFTER THEM.

ZOOM

W-WAIT UP!

GR

ZOOM ZOOM

FOR SHORT BURSTS, YEAH.

YOU COULD FLY ALL ALONG?

SORRY... THAT WAS SLOPPY.

YOU JUST HAAAD TO GO AND LET HIM GRAB YOU EVEN AFTER MY WARNING ABOUT HIS ABILITY?

TMP

TMP

MEANING, THAT ONE HE FIRED OFF WAS BASICALLY NO DIFFERENT THAN IF YOU'D DONE IT.

RIGHT, I UNDERSTAND.

WELL, THE COPIED MOVES ARE JUST AS STRONG AS THE ORIGINALS.

BUT TELL ME HOW BEST TO FIGHT HIM.

HERE HE COMES!!

SAME GOES FOR PUNCHES AND KICKS! THEY'RE ALL JUST LIKE YOUR MOVES!

SO I MUST THINK OF IT AS FIGHTING AN EXACT COPY OF MYSELF.

WOR MP

SKE

SKE

SLAM

SKF

SKF

WHAM
WHAM
WHAM
WHAM

WHAM
WHAM
WHAM

ACK!

YOINK

YOU'VE GOT SOME NERVE, SHIMO-REKKA!

YOU DARE STEAL MY SIDEARM? IT'S AS IMPORTANT AS A GALACTIC AGENT'S LIFE!

OVER HERE, GALACTIC LOSER.

T T T T T
M M M M M
P P P P P

GIVE IT BACK!!

SHP

38

SKFFF

FWAHH

BWOOM!!!

YOU MIGHT'VE MENTIONED THAT SOONER!

DAMMIT...

FORGOT TO MENTION-- THAT GUY'S GOT INFINITE STAMINA. YOU CAN'T WEAR HIM DOWN.

39

KRASH

EEK!

BWOOM

GET IN, EVERYONE!

BOM

LET'S FOLLOW THEM!

YOU OKAY DOWN THERE?

C-CUE BALL!

GWAHH!

KAZOOM

42

WHOOSH

D-DAMMIT!!

GETTING BEATEN BY MY OWN TECHNIQUES...

JUST TRY TO HOLD OUT!

SORRY, BUT I DON'T THINK I'LL LAST THAT LONG.

HE'LL BE BACK TO NORMAL AFTER 30 MINUTES!

KAWHAP

44

OOH, IT'S SON GOKU'S BOY!

!

ARE YOU OKAY, PICCOLO?

POW

SON GOKU AND MERUS TRAIN IN A SPECIAL DIMENSION CUT OFF FROM THE OUTSIDE WORLD, ONE WHERE TIME FLOWS DIFFERENTLY.

WHAM
WHAM
WHAM
WHAM

KA THUD

HFF!

HFF!

HFF!

I EXPECT YOU WERE IN AN EXTREME CRISIS WHEN IT FIRST ACTIVATED?

DARN ...

NOW I'M KINDA DOUBTING THAT I ACTUALLY EVER MANAGED TO USE ULTRA INSTINCT...

FOR SURE. IT WAS A MATTER OF LIFE AND DEATH.

YOU MEAN, I GOTTA BE PREPARED TO DIE DURING THIS TRAINING?

THEN THE QUICKEST WAY TO ACHIEVE IT AGAIN IS TO REPLICATE THOSE CONDITIONS.

THEN YOU'D BETTER COME AT ME TO KILL.

FINE...

YES. EXACTLY.

PLANET YARDRAT

I'M STARTING TO REGRET EVER COMING TO THIS ROCK...

DAMMIT...

FIRST, YOU MUST ACHIEVE BALANCE IN BODY AND MIND.

YOUR SPIRIT IS EVEN LESS STABLE THAN GOKU'S WAS.

HEY... HOW MANY MORE DAYS OF THIS?

YOUR BALANCE IS ALL DISRUPTED, AGAIN.

UGH... GRR...

BY THE WAY, GOKU WAS UP THERE FOR 150 DAYS.

FOR 150 DAYS?!

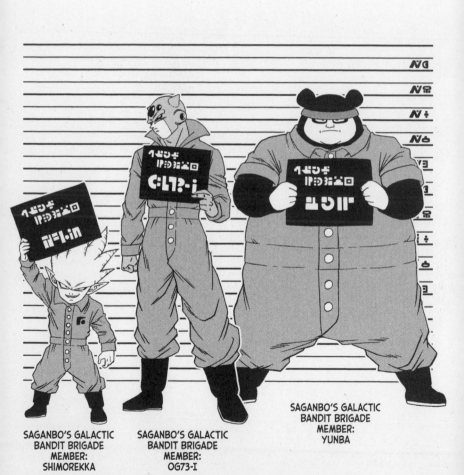

SAGANBO'S GALACTIC
BANDIT BRIGADE
MEMBER:
SHIMOREKKA

SAGANBO'S GALACTIC
BANDIT BRIGADE
MEMBER:
OG73-I

SAGANBO'S GALACTIC
BANDIT BRIGADE
MEMBER:
YUNBA

DRAGON BALL SUPER

CHAPTER 54:
GOHAN VS. SEVEN-THREE

VMMM

BOOM
BOOM
BOOM
BOOM

SKWEEE

GOHAN
!!

THERE
!!

BWAM

SEVEN-
THREE!!

!! SLAM

I KNOW YOUR MOVES BETTER THAN JUST ABOUT ANYONE, PICCOLO.

WELL DONE, GOHAN!

TMP

AND I'VE GOT MIXED FEELINGS ABOUT YOU BEATING A COPY OF ME THAT EASILY.

RIGHT!

NOW GET OUT THERE AND END THIS.

FWEW

!

FWOOMP

...!

NOW YOU'RE A GIANT, HUH?

BWO OMF

RRMMMM

TH-THE HECK?!

IT'S THAT OTHER GUY!

SHAKA

SHAKA

!

!

POW

POW

WH-AM!

...

UGH!

!TH UD

HUH?

ZOOM

DON'T QUIT ON ME NOW!

HEY!! SEVEN-THREE!

AND **THAT** GUY'S THE ONE WE SHOULDA HAD OUR MAN COPY.

GUESS OUR DATA FOR THIS PLANET WAS SUPER OUTDATED.

WHAT'S GOING ON, SHIMO-REKKA?

TOM

SHOOM

WHATEVER IT TAKES, GET YOUR HAND AROUND THAT GUY'S NECK!

LISTEN, SEVEN-THREE.

VERY WELL.

WOR

MP

DEFINITELY SOMEONE WE CAN COUNT ON. SAME AS ALWAYS.

PIC-COLO!

TMP

TOMP TOMP

YEAH.

GOHAN SHOWED UP, HUH?

SHOOM

SHOOM

...ME...

KA...

SMASH

...ME...

HA...

72

HUH?

UGH!

...!!

W-WHERE'S THE BOOM?

HMM?

H-HE ATE IT...

HE ATE
THE CHI
BLAST!

HAAH!

LOOK!
MORO
!!

GULP

FWP

HE HAD
MORO'S
POWERS
IN STOCK
!!

IN
STOCK?
YOU
NEVER
SAID
ANYTHING
ABOUT
THAT!

YEAH,
WELL, HE
CAN SWITCH
TO OTHER
COPIED
ABILITIES,
STORING UP
TO THREE
IDENTITIES
AT A TIME!!

WHAT'S
THAT
MEAN
...?

HE'S GONNA ABSORB ENERGY!

TAKE HIM DOWN BEFORE HE CAN !!

THIS IS BAD !!

WHAT NOW?

TCH!

ZOOM

BWOOSH

!!

FLK

KRAK
KRAK

FUNSH

BWODOSH

FWK

GAHH!!

...!!

WHAT'S ALL THAT ABOUT?!

WE CAN'T GET CLOSE!!

SO Y'SEE, CAPTAIN, WE HAD TO RESORT TO THAT. SORRY.

HMPH... CLOSE ONE, HUH? NEVER THOUGHT WE'D NEED OUR SECRET WEAPON SO SOON.

FINISH UP THERE QUICK AND GET BACK HERE.

...

IS THAT SO?

WHAT? THEY ALREADY MADE USE OF MY COPIED ABILITIES?

APOLOGIES, LORD MORO.

BUT I DON'T LIKE MY NECK GETTING TOUCHED ALL THE TIME. I DON'T WANT HIM EMPLOYING IT FOR JUST ANYTHING.

COPYING... A USEFUL POWER...

SORRY, THEY WERE SUPPOSED TO BE USED AS A LAST RESORT...

WE CAN CHECK IT OUT FROM HERE, ACTUALLY.

I ASSUME IT'S BEING PUT TO GOOD USE?

PROJECT THE LIVE FEED HERE, QUOITUR.

SURE.

YOU GOT IT!

SHIMO-REKKA, SWITCH TO MONITOR MODE.

HUFF!

HUFF!

HUFF!

HUFF!

BWOOM

F-FEELING DRAINED...

IT DOES COME AS A SURPRISE THAT EARTH IS HOME TO BEINGS STRONGER THAN MY GUYS.

RIGHT.

YES.

DOES THIS HAVE A TIME LIMIT AS WELL?

WHICH IS WHY THEY GOTTA END THIS QUICK.

THEY'VE EVOLVED QUITE A BIT SINCE THEN...

EARTH...? TEN MILLION YEARS AGO IT WAS A PLANET OF MERE MONKEYS.

POW POW

SLASH

SMAK SMAK

TOO BAD FOR YOU, BEING STRONGER DOESN'T ALWAYS NET YOU THE WIN.

GUH HUH HUH...

HEE HEE HEE...

GAAAAH!!

POW POW POW

SLAM

G-GOHAN!!

GAH!!

OH... THEM.

THE SAIYANS WHO WERE ON NAMEK.

...GOKU AND VEGETA WILL MAKE SURE YOU GO DOWN.

EVEN IF WE DIE TODAY...

GOKU? VEGETA? WHO'RE THEY?

?

WHAT ABOUT THEM?

TRAINING, YOU SAY?

YOU WON'T GET YOUR WAY, Y'KNOW!

RIGHT NOW THEY'RE TRAINING TO BEAT YOU PUNKS!

GOKU... VEGETA... SO THEY WERE THE GALACTIC PATROL MEMBERS ON NAMEK.

DID YOU HEAR THAT, LORD MORO?

POW POW POW

WHAM

WAIT.

WE'RE TAKING OFF.

PULL EVERYONE BACK FROM THIS PLANET.

SURE.

IF WE LET THEM RUN FREE, IT COULD COME BACK TO BITE US.

RIGHT. I THOUGHT THEY JUST TURNED TAIL FOR GOOD BACK THEN... BUT THEY'VE STILL GOT SOME FIGHT LEFT IN THEM. WHO KNEW?

THOSE TWO ARE SUPPOSEDLY TRAINING.

!

WHY NOT JUST GO AND EAT EARTH FIRST?

86

...THEY WILL DELIVER ME FAR GREATER ENERGY IF I ONLY WAIT A SPELL.

WHICH MEANS...

THE GALACTIC PATROL NO LONGER POSES A THREAT, SO WE NEED NOT REMAIN HIDDEN FROM THEM.

YOU GOT IT.

ONCE THE ONES CALLED GOKU AND VEGETA RETURN WITH MORE ENERGY THAN EVER, I SHALL CONSUME THEM AND THEIR PRECIOUS EARTH.

...TELL THOSE THREE TO RETREAT FROM EARTH.

FOR NOW...

HUH?

WE'LL BE BACK IN GALACTIC CYCLE 7, SO DON'T EVEN THINK OF RUNNING.

....!

Y'SEE, THIS PLANET'S TECH IS TOTALLY PRIMITIVE, SO IT'S GONNA TAKE TIME! YOU GOTTA WAIT UNTIL AT LEAST CYCLE 8!

BUT THEY'LL NEVER MAKE IT BACK BY CYCLE 7, SHIMO-REKKA!

IN EARTH TIME, ABOUT 20 DAYS.

H-HOW LONG DOES THAT GIVE US?

PHEW!

THAT LONG? FOR REAL?

I'LL LET LORD MORO KNOW.

FINE.

90

ZWOOM

KACHK

SKWEEZ

SHOOP

POP

LATER.

TMp

...

KOFF KOFF

KOFF KOFF

GOHAN! YOU OKAY?

WE'RE SAFE FOR NOW... I THINK?

AND TAKE IT EASY. DENDE CAN PATCH YOU RIGHT UP. HIM, OR A SENZU BEAN.

DON'T SWEAT IT! WE WOULD'VE REALLY BEEN IN TROUBLE WITHOUT YOU HERE.

SORRY, I LET THEM GET AWAY.

NICE GOING JACO!

YOU BOUGHT US AN EXTRA MONTH AND THEN SOME?

IN TWO MONTHS.

SO WHEN ARE THEY ACTUALLY RETURNING, JACO?

...

I MEAN, I CAN'T GO DYING BEFORE THAT ONE ANIME MOVIE COMES OUT NEXT MONTH.

YOU'RE ALIVE!!

BUL- MA!

ZOOM

GUYS !!

NEWS OF MORO'S IMPENDING TRIP TO EARTH REACHED MERUS VIA GALACTIC PATROL HQ.

UNDER- STOOD. WE WILL TRAVEL TO EARTH IN TWO MONTHS' TIME.

HOW- EVER, THE COUNTDOWN BEGAN FOR THIS GRAVE THREAT'S NEXT VISIT.

AND SO, EARTH WAS SAFE FROM DANGER FOR THE TIME BEING.

IT SEEMS ALL IS WELL, THOUGH. THANK GOODNESS AGENT JACO WAS THERE FOR THEM.

YES.

GOTCHA! BUT THEY SAID THE BAD GUYS ARE GONNA COME BACK?

MORO'S PALS SHOWED UP ON EARTH?!

HUH?!

IT GIVES US SIX MONTHS IN HERE. I FEEL SORRY FOR THE PLANETS THAT WILL BE SACRIFICED IN THE MEANTIME, BUT ASSURING MORO'S CAPTURE WHEN THE TIME COMES IS OUR TOP PRIORITY.

TWO MONTHS... THAT'S MORE TIME THAN WE THOUGHT, HUH?

YES.

MY BELLY'S FULL, SO LET'S GET RIGHT BACK TO IT!

WELL, FINE!

THAT MEANS MY TRAINING'S GOTTA PAY OFF, OR ELSE.

HUH? WHIS SAID THE SAME THING.

I CAN EAT, OR NOT EAT. IT'S ALL THE SAME TO ME.

I JUST REALIZED... I'VE NEVER SEEN YOU EAT. DON'TCHA EVER GET HUNGRY?

THE FOOD HERE'S KINDA MEH.

IF IT'S THE SAME TO YOU, THEN MAYBE I WON'T EAT EITHER.

DASH

DASH

APOLO-
GIES
FOR THE
SUDDEN
REQUEST.

WHIS?

NOW,
HOW
CAN
I HELP
YOU...

SO
VERY
SORRY
TO
MAKE
YOU
WAIT.

96

WELL, WHAT BUSINESS DID YOU HAVE WITH ME?

I AM DEEPLY ASHAMED FOR IT.

I PRESUME YOU ARE AWARE THAT OUR UNIVERSE IS ONCE AGAIN IN DISCORD?

GRAND PRIEST.

UNIVERSE 7 IS CERTAINLY A RESTLESS ONE.

IT SEEMS THAT WAY.

JUST SO.

I WOULD NEVER. WE ANGELS MUST MAINTAIN NEUTRALITY, SIDING WITH NEITHER GOOD NOR EVIL.

THEN WHAT WOULD YOU ASK OF ME?

I DON'T SUPPOSE YOU INTEND TO ASK FOR YOUR UNIVERSE TO BE SAVED?

YOU ARE AWARE, THEN?

THE MATTER OF MERUS, I SUPPOSE.

THERE IS SOMETHING I WISH TO CONFIRM CONCERNING OUR ANGEL LAWS...

SAGANBO'S
GALACTIC BANDIT
BRIGADE LEADER:
SAGANBO

DRAGON BALL SUPER

CHAPTER 55: MERUS'S TRUE IDENTITY

I DISPATCHED MY TRAINEE ANGEL, MERUS, TO UNIVERSE 7 SO THAT HE MIGHT LEARN ABOUT THE WAY OF THINGS AND BROADEN HIS PERSPECTIVE.

HIS ENLISTING IN THE GALACTIC PATROL SEEMED A DECENT CHOICE, AS IT WOULD ALLOW HIM TO OBSERVE THE SIDE OF GOOD AND VIRTUE, BUT, ALAS...

BEYOND THAT SINGLE LAW, THERE ARE NO RESTRICTIONS ON WHAT WE CAN OR CANNOT DO.

WE ANGELS MUST ALWAYS ACT IMPARTIALLY.

INDEED.

ANY FURTHER INVOLVEMENT WOULD MAKE HIM IN VIOLATION OF OUR CODE.

JUST SO.

HE SEEMS TO HAVE GAINED A BIAS?

MEANING?

...

MIGHT YOU ALLOW ME TO COLLECT MERUS AND DEAL WITH HIM ON MY OWN?

GRAND PRIEST.

...I SHALL HAVE TO END MERUS'S TENURE IN THE MORTAL REALM.

AS HE IS PUSHING THE LIMIT...

100

YES. IT IS AS YOU SAY.

AND AT THE MOMENT, ALL HE IS DOING IS **TRAINING** GOKU... NO MORE THAN THAT.

HIS ACTIONS WITH THE GALACTIC PATROL HAVE BEEN LIMITED TO FIGHTING WITH MORTAL WEAPONS-- HE HASN'T USED HIS ANGEL ABILITIES.

EVEN I HAVE TAKEN IT UPON MYSELF TO TRAIN MORTALS.

HE HAS COME PERILOUSLY CLOSE, BUT HE HAS NOT YET VIOLATED OUR LAWS.

VERY WELL.

AM I THAT TRANSPARENT?

HO HO HO...

ONLY BECAUSE YOU CRAVED THE FOOD ON EARTH.

BUT DO KEEP A CLOSE EYE ON THAT ONE.

MUCH OBLIGED.

I LEAVE MERUS IN YOUR CARE.

GO ON.

UNDER-STOOD.

...I DO NOT WISH TO LOSE AN ANGEL.

TROUBLE-MAKER OR NOT...

KZZZZT

KZZZZT

PLANET YARDRAT

WITH NO WAY TO COMMUNICATE, IRICO AND VEGETA COULDN'T RECEIVE UPDATES.

YARDRAT FALLS OUTSIDE OF THE GALACTIC PATROL'S JURISDICTION.

WHAT'S GOING ON OUT IN THE GALAXY...? I SURE HOPE EVERYONE'S OKAY...

DARN... I STILL CAN'T GET AHOLD OF HQ.

KNNT

WAIT. THAT SHIP...

HMM?

NOOSH

ONE OF ELDER PYBARA'S SIGNATURE MOVES. PRETTY GREAT, HUH?

WAS THAT...

...A HEALING TECHNIQUE?

EWK

!

SHAH

AND I CAN LEARN TO PERFORM SUCH A MOVE?

FIRST, THE MOST FUNDAMENTAL BASICS-- I WILL TEACH YOU INSTANT TELEPORTATION.

TCH...

THAT'S HIGH-LEVEL STUFF, AND YOU'RE NOT THERE JUST YET.

HA HA HA, DON'T GET AHEAD OF YOURSELF.

INSTANT TELEPORTATION IS ONLY THE BASICS?

WHAT CAN I DO AT THIS POINT THEN?

KABOOM

I-I'M SENSING WICKED SPIRITS ON OUR PLANET!!

RMMMB!

WHAT THE--?

!

YIKES... WE'VE GOT UN-PLEASANT GUESTS.

ZOOM

VEGETA !!

LORD MORO OUGHT TO KNOW ABOUT THIS...

MORO WON'T BE MAKING A MEAL OF THIS PLANET.

THAT'S YUZUN-- ONE OF SAGANBO'S MINIONS.

HO HO HO! SO YOU'VE FLED ALL THE WAY TO THIS ROCK?

OH, YOU ARE... YES, THE GALACTIC PATROL MEMBER FROM NAMEK!

NOT ON MY WATCH.

BWOOOM

WITH NO WARNING ...?

H-HOW DARE YOU?!

KNOCK THAT OFF! DON'T GO WRECKING OUR PLANET!

FWK

FWK

WHAT WAS THAT...?

W...

WHAT?

CARE TO EXPLAIN?

GOOD THING NOBODY ACTUALLY LIVES IN THIS CITY, BUT STILL.

BEFORE YOUR TRAINING HERE, YOUR BODY AND SPIRIT WERE SO OFF-BALANCE THAT YOU COULDN'T PROJECT YOUR OWN POWER VERY WELL.

YOU JUST WITNESSED YOUR OWN NASCENT POWER.

BY LEAPS AND BOUNDS.

SURE HAVE.

MEANING I'VE ALREADY GROWN STRONGER SINCE I ARRIVED...?

114

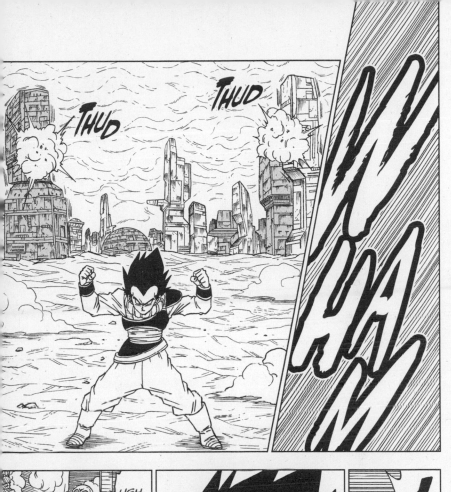

THUD

THUD

WHAM

UGH...

TWITCH

TWITCH

!

TRY YOU?
I BELIEVE
I JUST DID.

...WILL
YOU BE
KILLING
...?

SORRY,
I DIDN'T
QUITE
CATCH
THAT. WHO
EXACTLY
...

SKF

SKF

122

YOU'RE NO MATCH FOR ME, SO JUST STOP.

THIS IS FUTILE.

NOT A CHANCE...

TCH...

I TOLD HIM NOT TO WRECK THE PLACE...

BUT IF YOU SURRENDER AND RETURN TO THE GALACTIC PRISON, I WON'T HAVE TO KILL YOU.

I CAN'T ALLOW YOU TO RUN BACK TO MORO.

KRMBL

WHOA!!

COULD THAT BE THE PLANET YOU CALL HOME?

OH? THAT SURE GOT YOU WORKED UP.

IT'S A PLACE CALLED EARTH.

HMPH! DON'T YOU FRET-- LORD MORO'S NEXT TARGET ISN'T THIS PLANET.

VOOM

?

WHAT?!

!

ANYHOW, I'LL BE TAKING MY LEAVE NOW.

DID I HEAR THAT RIGHT? EARTH'S ON THE MENU?!

SHWP

TMP

SO THAT SCUM HAS SET HIS SIGHTS ON EARTH, HAS HE?!

KAZOOSH

TMP

TOMP

THAT ONE CALLED VEGETA.

I SEE. HE TRULY HAS GROWN MORE POWERFUL.

WHAT? IT CAN'T BE.

ON THE PLANET YUZUN VENTURED TO, YES. THOUGH YUZUN IS NOW DEAD.

YOU FOUND HIM?

!

IN THAT CASE, I SHALL STOCK UP AND REACH THE UPPER LIMITS OF MY POWER BEFORE TRAVELING TO EARTH.

HEH HEH HEH... WHAT A DELIGHTFUL DEVELOPMENT.

WHEN HE TRANSFORMS, HE'S SUPPOSED TO BE UNBEATABLE...

SAGANBO! FIND MORE SUITABLE PLANETS FOR ME.

Y-YOU GOT IT.

ASSUMING SUCH LIMITS EVEN EXIST.

HA... HA HA...

MEANWHILE, GOKU AND VEGETA'S TRAINING ALSO PROGRESSED, UNTIL, AT LAST, TWO MONTHS HAD PASSED.

LEADING UP TO HIS ATTACK ON EARTH, MORO CONTINUED TO DEVOUR PLANETS THROUGHOUT THE GALAXY.

LET US SPAR ONCE MORE BEFORE TAKING OFF FOR EARTH.

TIME IS NEARLY UP.

I'LL JUST HAFTA USE EVERYTHING I'VE LEARNED IN HERE.

SOUNDS GOOD.

I WON'T HOLD BACK EITHER.

SKF

SKF

WOOM
WOOM
WOOM

RMMBL

BWOOM

FWOOP

WE'RE OUTSIDE AGAIN!

H-HEY.

WHAT?

...

...QUITE ENOUGH.

THAT'S...

FSSH

BROTHER.

B...

IT'S YOU, WHIS!

HUH?

BROTHER?

HMM?

SO YOU CAUGHT WIND OF WHAT I WAS UP TO?

IT HAS BEEN AGES, MERUS.

I KNEW YOU WERE WEIRD, BUT YOU'RE AN ANGEL, MERUS?

ANGELS?!

...BETWEEN ANGELS.

I'M AFRAID THERE ARE NO SECRETS...

APOLO-GIES.

CLASHING AGAINST EACH OTHER AT FULL STRENGTH CONSTITUTES A BATTLE.

TRAINING CAN ONLY BE JUST THAT-- *TRAINING.*

YES.

Y-YOU KNEW...

...WAS YOUR PLAN TO TRAVEL TO EARTH AND DO BATTLE AGAINST MORO.

EVEN MORE EGREGIOUS...

I APOLOGIZE FOR KEEPING IT FROM YOU...

THAT EXPLAINS A LOT, MERUS.

JUST SO.

OHH, RIGHT. ANGELS AREN'T ALLOWED TO FIGHT EXCEPT IN TRAINING, RIGHT?

WHAT HAPPENS IF YOU GUYS DO FIGHT?

BUT WAIT...

...WITHOUT A TRACE.

ANGELS WHO BREAK OUR CODE ARE ERADICATED...

THERE IS NO WAY AROUND THIS TRUTH-- SUCH IS THE NATURE OF ANGELS.

IT IS THE ONLY MEANS BY WHICH AN ANGEL CAN BE REMOVED FROM EXISTENCE.

I THOUGHT ANGELS COULDN'T DIE!

ERADI- WHAT?! LIKE, POOF?!

HUH?

UNDER-STOOD.

...

YEESH...

FLK

HENCEFORTH, I WILL BE RESPONSIBLE FOR YOU.

ON THAT NOTE, I'VE COME TO INFORM YOU THAT YOUR TIME IN THE MORTAL REALM IS OVER, MERUS.

MERUS...

FWOOM

BE GRATEFUL THAT I'M NOT DRAGGING YOU RIGHT BACK TO THE GRAND PRIEST.

TAP

FLK

I'M ONLY SORRY I COULDN'T SEE THIS THROUGH WITH YOU.

GOKU...

! FWOOM TAP

I'LL FIGURE SOMETHING OUT.

SURE.

I HAVE FAITH THAT YOU WILL DEFEAT MORO.

YES.

IT'S BACK TO THE HEAVENLY REALM WITH YOU.

142

TWNKL

KAZOOSH!!

THANKS, MERUS.

UNTIL NEXT TIME, GOKU.

COME BAAACK, WHIS!!

WAAAIT!! I CAN'T DO IT!!

HOLD UP! I GOTTA PILOT THAT THING BACK TO EARTH MYSELF?!

ANYHOO... BETTER GET MYSELF BACK TO EARTH.

...

SAGANBO'S
GALACTIC BANDIT
BRIGADE MEMBER:
YUZUN

DRAGON BALL SUPER

CHAPTER 56: WARRIORS OF EARTH ASSEMBLE

EARTH
...

HEY, NEW RECRUITS!! LOOK SHARP!

CRUD... WHY'D THEY GOTTA PUT ME IN CHARGE OF EARTH? OF ALL THE ROTTEN LUCK.

IT'S FINALLY MY CHANCE TO SHINE!

IT'S BEEN SO LONG... I HOPE I CAN STILL FIGHT.

...

WE'RE PRETTY MUCH THE VETS OF PROTECTING THE EARTH...

TCH! NEW RECRUITS?

ARE GOKU AND VEGETA STILL NOT HERE, JACO?

YEAH. WON'T BE LONG NOW.

IT'S FINALLY TIME.

...I'M SURE THEY'LL SHOW.

BUT GIVEN THE BEEF THOSE TWO HAVE WITH MORO...

HUH?! THAT'S BAD!

I SENT GOKU A HEADS-UP, BUT WE'VE GOT NO CLUE WHERE VEGETA IS.

SO GLAD YOU'RE OKAY, PAL...

HE'S BEEN FAST ASLEEP SINCE HIS LAST BATTLE.

ZZZ

ZZZ

BOO!

VRRRM

GALACTIC PATROL OR NOT, YOU'LL BE ANSWERING TO ME IF YOU TRY KIDNAPPING BOO AGAIN!

S-SORRY ABOUT THAT.

LIKE THAT ONE?

A BIG MOTHER-SHIP SHAPED LIKE A TOP WITH LOTS OF LITTLE SCOUT SHIPS.

WHAT DOES MORO'S SPACE-SHIP LOOK LIKE?

ZOOSH

BWOOOSH

SLAM SLAM

FWAH

WH-WHO'S THAT?!

!!

TOMP

154

YOU AGAIN?

TMP

HNNGH...

I'VE BEEN TRAINING HARD!

I'M NOT THE SAME MAN AS BEFORE!

FWAP

FINE BY ME, LET'S SETTLE THIS NOW.

GUH HUH HUH ...

ZOOM

YUNBA! WE DON'T GIVE A CRAP ABOUT THIS DUEL OF YOURS, SO WE'RE GONNA GO WRECK SOME OTHER PLACE.

SURE. GO ON, THEN.

...

DASH

DASH DASH!

Y'CAN'T GO RELYING ON YOUR OLD MASTER FOR EVERYTHING. I'M BETTING YOU CAN HANDLE THIS CHUMP ALONE.

KURI-RIN...

MUTEN RÔSHI... THIS GUY'S WAY FASTER THAN HE LOOKS, SO LET'S RUSH HIM TOGETHER!

HUH?!

MEAN-WHILE, I'LL GO WRANGLE THOSE NASTY BABES.

♪

BOING

!

KA POW

I AIN'T WAITING AROUND!

RMMBL

HAHH!!

POW POW POW

DARN YOU!!

OWWW!

HANG IN THERE, GUYS...

THERE'RE FIGHTS STARTING ALL OVER THE PLANET...

WE'VE GOT COMPANY TOO.

ALONE THIS TIME?

YOU WISH.

TMP

WHA--

HUH?

FWUNK

ZRM

!!

W-WHEN DID HE--

YOU PEOPLE ARE DUMB AS EVER, I SEE.

THAT MOVE CAME COURTESY OF AN INVISIBLE RACE.

TCH !!

ZRM

ZRM

I-IDIOT! YOU DROPPED YOUR GUARD AGAIN!

ANY TRAINING YOU MIGHT'VE DONE? ALL TOTALLY WORTHLESS NOW.

DAM-MIT!!

SINCE SEVEN-THREE COPIES YOU THE WAY YOU ARE RIGHT NOW.

LOOK, TEN...

THAT'S PICCOLO'S! THE FIGHTING MUST'VE STARTED BACK THERE TOO.

FWOOSH

EVEN WITH INFINITE STAMINA, IT'S NOT LIKE HE CAN RECOVER IMMEDIATELY.

170

KRK

B-BUT HOW?!

HOW'S THIS HAPPENING?!

SPLORCH

BRGL BRGL

WE WERE TOTALLY READY FOR HIM TO COPY OUR ABILITIES.

RRRIP

SWITCH OVER TO HIM!

SEVEN-THREE, THAT ONE GUY IS STRONG-ER.

VERY WELL.

HMPH! SOUNDS LIKE A BLUFF TO ME.

HUMM HUMM

TCH!

PEW PEW PEW PEW PEW PEW PEW PEW

GOHAN!

PEW

ZOOM

SPLOOSH

GOOD GOING, GOHAN!!

SEVEN-THREE CAN ONLY USE ONE SET OF POWERS AT A TIME...

...SO THERE'S NO WAY HE CAN DODGE ATTACKS FROM A DUO!

OF COURSE! COMBO MOVES!!

TH-THAT CAN'T BE!

WE'LL NEVER LOSE TO SOME COPYCAT.

SPLOOSH

SEEMS LIKE GOHAN AND PICCOLO'S TRAINING IS PAYING OFF.

UGH!

YOU LOOKED SO FREAKIN' WEAK...

DAMMIT...

GAH!

ACTUALLY, I'M ONE OF THE THREE STRONGEST EARTHLINGS AROUND.

AW, YOU THINK?

178

POW POW POW

RAHHHH!!

ZOOSH

ZOOM

POW WHAK WHAK

...

RIGHT!

BETTER ROUND THEM UP WHILE YOU CAN.

URRGH ...

THUD THUD THUD

TMP

...

I'M SENSING MORE RAMPAGING CONVICTS THAT WAY... LET'S HURRY!

RMMMMBL

DID WE GET HIM?!

HFF!

HE'LL RESORT TO MORO'S POWER AGAIN...

IF WE DON'T FINISH HIM OFF... HE'LL...

NO, NOT YET!

...

TMP

TMP

TMP

IT'LL BE FOR NOTHING IF WE END UP DEAD!!

C'MON! JUST USE IT ALREADY, SEVEN-THREE.

FWK

TMP

TMP

GET THEM! DRAIN THEIR ENERGY TILL THEY'RE DRY!!

FWP

THEY SAID HE'S GOT NO EMOTIONS... SO YEAH, PROBABLY.

WHICH ONE'S THAT SEVEN-ELEVEN GUY? WAS HE THE ONE I KICKED?

GAH!

WH- WHO'RE THEY?!

SINCE YOU ANDROIDS DON'T HAVE CHI.

YOU SURE YOU EVEN NEED US, PICCOLO?

YEAH, YOU'RE THE ONLY ONES WHO CAN FINISH THIS FIGHT.

WEIRD. SEEMS PRETTY WEAK TO ME.

...MY LOW EXPECTATIONS OF THEM.

TCH... PATHETIC. THESE USELESS FOOLS COULDN'T EVEN MEET...

KREEK

IT SEEMS LIKE A WHOLE BUNCH OF TOUGH FIGHTERS GATHERED ON EARTH, SOMEHOW...

APOLOGIES, LORD MORO.

NOW... WHO WILL BE FIRST ON MY MENU?

NO MATTER. THERE WOULD BE NO MEANING IN COMING ALL THIS WAY OTHERWISE.

ONE MORE TIME.

DAMMIT! IT FAILED...

ON YARDRAT

WFF!

WFF!

YES. THE FIGHTING STARTED NOT LONG AGO.

CAN YOU FEEL THE EARTH'S SPIRIT?

WAIT, VEGETA.

WELL? SHOULDN'T YOU RUSH OVER THERE?

NO POINT... NOT UNTIL I'VE MASTERED THIS TECHNIQUE...

FROM THE TOP, PYBARA.

NOW! ONCE MORE!

CUTTING IT CLOSE, HUH?

THERE'S STILL TIME.

BESIDES, MORO HASN'T JOINED THE BATTLE, YET.

IT'S ELDER! ELDER PYBARA!

...WAS A BIT LOST.

THAT-AWAY.

WHICH WAY IS EARTH?

MEAN-WHILE, GOKU...

TO BE CONTINUED!

WHAT NOW? GO ON, SPIT IT OUT.

LORD FREEZA!

LORD FREEZA!

AT THAT MOMENT, SOMEWHERE DEEP IN SPACE

BONUS MANGA

THE GALACTIC PRISON, YOU SAY?

APPARENTLY, ESCAPED CONVICTS FROM THE GALACTIC PRISON ARE RAVAGING THE PLANET THAT WAS TO BE OUR NEXT TARGET.

A-A THOUSAND APOLOGIES.

NOTHING GOOD CAN COME FROM MIXING WITH CRIMINALS.

C-CRIMINALS...?

...ALSO CRIMINALS...?

UM, AREN'T WE...

LET'S AVOID MEANINGLESS CONFLICT FOR NOW AND SIMPLY MOVE ON TO THE NEXT PLANET.

VERY WELL.

I HAVE HEARD THAT THE PRISONERS INCARCERATED THERE ARE AS NASTY AS THEY COME.

N-NASTY PRISONERS, LORD FREEZA?

PRECISELY AS BERRY-BLUE SAYS.

WE OCCUPY PLANETS AND EXTERMINATE THEIR INHABITANTS IN ORDER TO SELL THOSE PLANETS FOR A TIDY PROFIT TO RACES WHO HAVE LOST THEIR OWN HOMES. **WE ARE RUNNING A BUSINESS.**

WHAT DID YOU SAY?

KIKONO, WE ARE MOST CERTAINLY NOT CRIMINALS.

ACK... NOTHING. NEVER MIND.

IT'S A BIG UNIVERSE, OUT THERE.

THEN GET SEARCHING FOR OTHER PLANETS.

Y-YES, LORD FREEZA.

IS THAT A PROBLEM, KIKONO?

NOPE!

N...

YOU'RE READING THE WRONG WAY!

Dragon Ball Super reads from right to left, starting in the upper-right corner. Japanese is read from right to left, meaning that action, sound effects, and word-balloon order are completely reversed from English order.